AUSTRALIA REMEMBERS 5

Cameron Baird VC, MG

Dedicated, Courageous and Born to Lead

EAST TIMOR • IRAQ • AFGHANISTAN

BIG SKY PUBLISHING

www.bigskypublishing.com.au

ALLISON PATERSON

We acknowledge the traditional owners of country throughout Australia and recognise their continuing connection to land, waters and culture. We pay our respects to their Elders past, present and emerging.

Aboriginal and Torres Strait Islander readers are advised that this book contains images of people who have passed away.

A portion of the proceeds of this book will be donated to the charity Cam's Cause.

First published 2022

Big Sky Publishing Pty Ltd
PO Box 303, Newport, NSW 2106, Australia
Phone: 1300 364 611
Email: info@bigskypublishing.com.au
Web: www.bigskypublishing.com.au

Cover Design and Typesetting: Think Productions
Editing by Allison Marlow Paterson and Catherine McCullagh

A catalogue record for this book is available from the National Library of Australia

National Library of Australia Cataloguing-in-Publication entry
Author: Allison Paterson
Title: Australia Remembers 5: Cameron Baird VC, MG
Dedicated, Courageous and Born to Lead
978-1-922615-57-2 (HB)
978-1-922615-58-9 (PB)

Front cover images:
The photo of Cameron as a child is courtesy of the Baird family. Images of Cameron while serving in the Australian Defence Force are courtesy of the Department of Defence.

Dedication

For Cameron, his family and for all those who have served this country in times of war and in peacekeeping operations.

Contents

Chapter 1

COMMEMORATION – THE PEOPLE OF TODAY

Anzac Day and Remembrance Day are two special days of commemoration in Australia. On these days we remember, honour and thank all those who have fought to protect others or suffered in war and **conflict** in the past.

As Australians, we have many freedoms, including the right to go to school, to choose where we live, our jobs and our religion. But life can be different in other countries and, in some places in the world, there is conflict. When conflict breaks out the leaders of countries will try to resolve it in a peaceful way. Peaceful solutions are not always found, and this can lead to war.

Anzac Day service in Tewantin, 2012 (courtesy St Andrew's Anglican College).

FAST FACT

The Australian Defence Force (ADF) consists of the Australian Army, Royal Australian Navy (RAN) and Royal Australian Air Force (RAAF). The three organisations once worked separately but were united as the ADF in 1976.

DID YOU KNOW?

Commemoration means to honour the memory of an event, a group of people or a person by holding a service, ceremony or celebration. Special memorials or objects are also made to help us honour and remember.

Private Joshua Hetherington talks to an Afghan child in Uruzgan province, 2010 (AWM P11170.005).

DID YOU KNOW?

On Anzac Day and Remembrance Day we also recognise those who are serving our country in dangerous places today. Both days help us remember the sacrifice so many men and women have made for our freedom and safety.

An official portrait of Corporal Cameron Baird who was killed on active service in Afghanistan on 22 June 2013 (courtesy Department of Defence).

For over a century, Australian **servicemen and women** have served, been wounded or lost their lives in many conflicts around the world. Some of these conflicts occurred in the past, such as World War I, which was fought over 100 years ago, or World War II, now 80 years ago. But since the end of World War II members of the Australian Defence Force (ADF), the soldiers of the Australian Army, sailors of the Royal Australian Navy (RAN) and airmen and women of the Royal Australian Air Force (RAAF), have continued to fight in wars, serve as peacekeepers and help in times of disaster in many countries beyond Australia including Korea, Malaysia, Vietnam, Zimbabwe, Iran, Iraq, Namibia, Western Sahara, Cambodia, Somalia, Yugoslavia, Rwanda, Bougainville, East Timor, Solomon Islands, Indonesia, Fiji and Afghanistan.

Australian service personnel have made great sacrifices in recent conflicts. Cameron Baird, VC, MG was a courageous and dedicated Australian soldier who served in the conflict zones of East Timor, Iraq and Afghanistan. Cameron lost his life on 22 June 2013 while leading his team in a dangerous mission in Afghanistan. At the time of his death, Cameron was attempting to rescue a mate.

Chapter 2

CAMERON BAIRD

Cameron Baird was born on a cold winter's day in Burnie, Tasmania, on 7 June 1981.

When Cameron was three, his parents, Doug and Kaye, returned to Melbourne, the Victorian city in which they had grown up. Along with his nine-year-old brother Brendan, Cameron settled in the suburb of Gladstone Park where he spent the rest of his childhood.

The Baird family loved Australian Rules Football. Cameron's father had previously played with the Australian Football League team of Carlton. Doug encouraged both his sons to play and enjoy the sport, spending hours teaching his boys football skills. Cameron grew to love football as much as his dad loved the sport.

At Gladstone Views Primary School, Cameron excelled at many sports, including cricket and athletics. He grew taller and stronger than his classmates. By the time he was in Year Five, he was even taller than most of his teachers. Cameron was competitive and disciplined — he trained hard and he wanted to win. Yet, at Little Athletics, Cameron often gave away his medals and ribbons to others. He wanted his competitors and teammates to feel good about themselves too. Despite his many sporting achievements, Cameron didn't boast about his ability, not even when he became the Australian junior champion in discus and the Victorian junior champion in shot-put

Cameron was in Year One and six years old at the time of this photo (courtesy of the Baird family).

Cameron with his older brother Brendan in 1981 (courtesy of the Baird family).

Cameron's natural athletic ability began to shine at an early age (courtesy of the Baird family).

Cameron enjoyed all physical sports (courtesy of the Baird family).

Australian junior discus champion in 1993 (courtesy of the Baird family).

When Cameron was in Year Four, he was asked to join the school's football team, usually made up of Year Five and Six students. Teacher Andrew Harrison was the team coach at the time. He recognised that Cameron had exceptional skills and a natural ability to lead. It wasn't long before nine-year-old Cameron was being pushed forward by his older teammates to lead the team onto the field.

Cam impressed everyone from the moment he came to the first training session. A talent that I had not yet seen in school footy. Cameron was always quietly confident in his ability and thrived on the challenge and competitive nature of football … On his debut, the boys in grades five and six insisted Cam lead the school team onto the ground. Cameron would continue leading the team, as captain, for two more years … He proved to be a strong, motivational and inclusive leader from the outset. Cameron insisted that there be some team rules. The first was that all players would pass the ball off to the first Gladstone Views jumper they saw. Cam firmly believed that this rule would not only ensure that everyone was included in the game but would also raise the confidence and skill level of all players … Cameron's values and understandings around leadership, including strong communication skills, were established at an early age.

As a student Cameron was enthusiastically dedicated to the learning journey. Not content with simply applying himself, he always maintained a sharp focus with attention to detail. A skill he maintained throughout his life. (Andrew Harrison, The Art of Sacrifice)

Cameron was always proud to lead his mates. Here Cameron celebrates winning the premiership cup in 1993. With him on his immediate right are his friends Daniel Carroll and Rick Green (courtesy of the Baird family).

Cameron in Year Six (courtesy of the Baird family).

The Year Six class of Gladstone Views Primary School when Andrew Harrison was Cameron's class teacher (courtesy of the Baird family).

In Year Five, Cameron continued to practise his skills and spent his summer holidays kicking the footy with his dad. He returned to school and announced to Mr Harrison that he was going to do a lot better that year and so would the team. Cameron was right.

At the end of the year, he just missed out on being selected in the Victorian Primary Schoolboys side. He needed to work on kicking and passing the ball with his left side, rather than his dominant right side. Cameron persevered and continued to practise. He returned after the summer holidays and again announced he had improved.

That year the Gladstone Views team reached the semi-finals. At three-quarter time they were losing. Andrew Harrison told Cameron the team could still win but it was up to him to make the difference. The team won by a point. Cameron always regarded this game as his greatest football moment — he had played in a team with childhood mates and led them to victory.

Cameron also fulfilled his goal — he was selected for and captained the Victorian Schoolboys team which won the national championship. This team included Jonathan Brown, a player who later captained the Brisbane Lions of the Australian Football League.

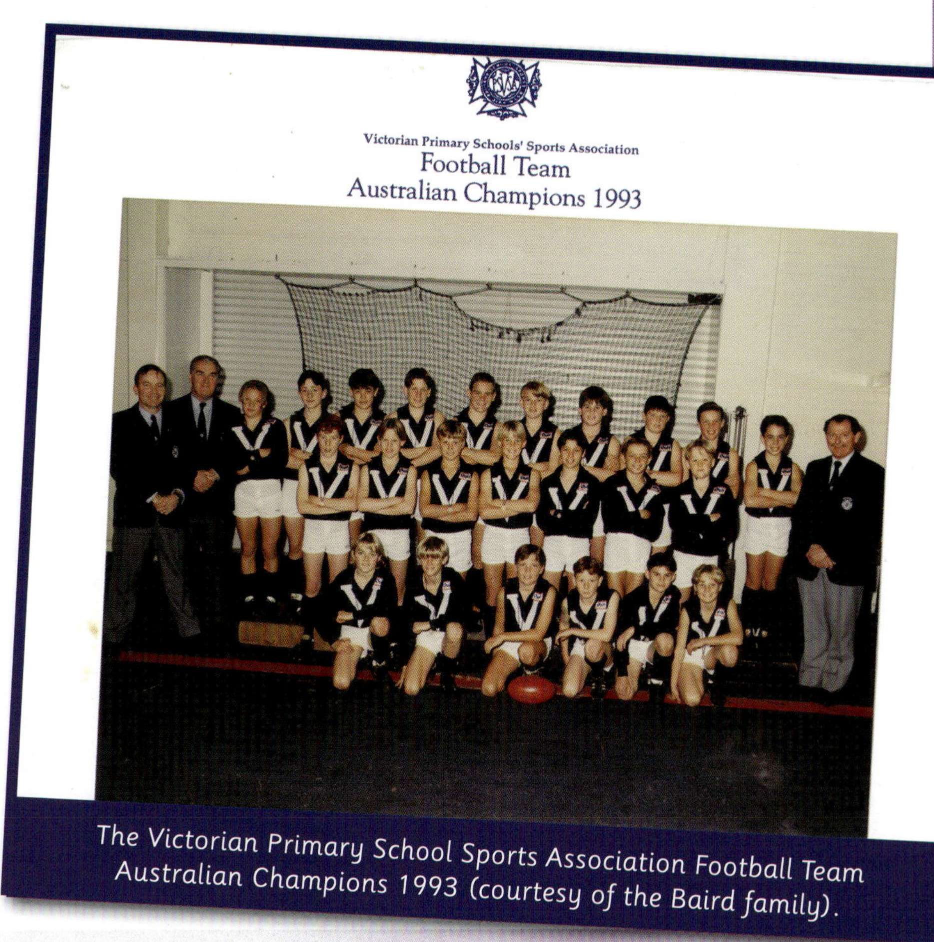

The Victorian Primary School Sports Association Football Team Australian Champions 1993 (courtesy of the Baird family).

It was also in Year Six that Cameron visited the Australian War **Memorial** for the first time on a school trip to Canberra. Andrew Harrison recalls that Cameron showed great interest in the Commemorative Courtyard and the Roll of Honour which records the names of the more than 102,000 men and women who have given their lives in the service of Australia. Cameron remarked that these servicemen and women must have been very brave.

Darby Hipwell (courtesy of the Baird Family).

The Inaugural School Sports Victoria Corporal Cameron Baird VC MG Award

Darby Hipwell was the 2015 winner of the Inaugural School Sports Victoria Corporal Cameron Baird, VC, MG Award, established in honour of Cameron. It recognises exemplary leadership, strength of character, ability to inspire others, courage and commitment. The recipient is also awarded a number 4 Australian Rules Football jumper, the same number Cameron wore as captain of the team.

Darby later wrote to Cameron's parents:

I thought I would write to you a short letter to explain how significant it was to me to receive the Cameron Baird medal. Cameron sounded like an amazing person … brave, courageous, kind and caring … Cameron and you have inspired me not only in my football but in my life.

What is a memorial? Are there memorials in your loca area? Who or what events do they commemorate?

DID YOU KNOW?

The Australian War Memorial in Canberra was opened on 11 November 1941, during World War II. It is a memorial to all those who have served Australia or suffered during war and conflict. It is also a museum in which war relics are displayed and an archive where important documents from past wars are collected.

The Roll of Honour in the Commemorative Courtyard of the Australian War Memorial.

In Year Six, Cameron visited Canberra for the first time. This image shows his class at Government House (courtesy of the Baird family).

Australian War Memorial, Canberra, ACT.

Chapter 3

TEAMWORK – CAMERON AS A TEENAGER

Cameron's dedication to Australian Rules Football continued throughout his teen years. His other passion was his guitar, a gift from his parents in 1991. As well as polishing his football skills he now practised his guitar with the same dedication, even taking it to school to play at lunchtime. Later, his guitar would travel with him across the world during his service in various conflicts.

Selected in the regional team of Strathmore Football Club, Cameron excelled as captain of the U/16 team. Despite breaking his arm and playing only six games in the season, he was awarded the best and fairest trophy. His attitude to his teammates was the same as in primary school — he showed compassion and helped the younger and smaller players. He was regarded as courageous and as a great team player.

I had the privilege of growing up with Cameron. I can reflect on some key characteristics that identified Cameron as a champion, legend and a role model from an early age … He knew exactly who he was and what path he wanted to take long before he was an adult. Whether it was AFL football or the military, Cameron's life objective was to be the best version of himself. He wanted to leave nothing behind.

Cameron always held himself with a lot of respect and showed others the same courtesy. He was a loyal friend and had a lot of empathy for other people. Cameron looked out for smaller kids at school who may have been picked on, and cared for those whose confidence was down, giving them a much-needed pat on the back or high five. He protected his team on the footy field and would give away an easy goal to a teammate to give them the encouragement they needed to improve in their game. Cameron did it all. (Chris Dyer, Cameron's classmate and friend, The Art of Sacrifice).

The Rising Sun Badge is the emblem of the Australian Army.

Cameron in Year 12 (courtesy of the Baird family).

Cameron completed Year 12 in 1999. He was a respectful student and his teachers admired his passion for his greatest love — football. Everyone thought that Cameron was destined for a career as a football player in a national Australian Football League (AFL) team. But the unexpected happened. Cameron injured his shoulder while playing football and required surgery. Despite recovering, the injury affected his training and, later that year, it dashed his dreams of being drafted into an AFL team

Cameron was bitterly disappointed, but he didn't let self-pity take control. He decided to use his athletic strengths, his courage, his ability to work in a team and his leadership skills in another way. He joined the Australian Army.

Cameron was a favourite son at Gladstone Park High and all the teachers and fellow students who came in contact with him held him in the highest regard … I was so impressed with his humility and empathy for others. He knew his ability and never for a moment displayed anything but a selfless attitude. (Len Hannah, former teacher at Gladstone Park Secondary College and coach of the Calder Cannons courtesy Baird family).

Cameron on the day he enlisted in the Australian Army. (courtesy of the Baird family).

DID YOU KNOW?

The Australian Army has its origins in the first armed forces of colonial times. In 1901, the Australian colonies became a federated nation. Two years after Federation, the armies of the colonies combined to become the Commonwealth Military Forces, later named the Australian Military Forces. These forces were only allowed to serve on Australian soil. Two volunteer forces were created for service overseas in World War I and World War II. These were known as the Australian Imperial Force (AIF). In 1947, the Australian Regular Army was formed and was supported by the Citizen Military Force, now known as the Army Reserve. The name Australian Army was first introduced in 1980.

Chapter 4

To Serve His Country

In January 2000, Cameron began his training as a soldier at the Army Recruit Training Centre at Kapooka, near Wagga Wagga, New South Wales. He wasn't the first of his family to serve his country. Cameron's great-grandfather, George Baird, had served with the Australian Imperial Force (AIF) in World War I and his grandfather, John Baird, was a member of the Second AIF in World War II. His brother Brendan had also been a member of the Army Reserve.

At first, Cameron found it difficult to adjust to the disciplined lifestyle of the ADF, but within a few weeks he wrote home to his parents:

I was never put on this earth to play football or anything else, I was meant to be a soldier.

The entrance to the Army Recruit Training Centre, Kapooka (courtesy Department of Defence).

He was now as committed to becoming a soldier as he had been to becoming a football player. He graduated from Kapooka on 18 February 2000 after being named the Most Outstanding Soldier in his platoon.

After graduating, Cameron began his training as an infantry soldier. His determination to be the best meant that, once again, he excelled. At the end of the course, he applied to join the 4th Battalion of the Royal Australian **Regiment** (4 RAR). This regiment was developing as a commando **unit**. Commando soldiers are trained for fast-moving raids against enemy forces. With his athletic ability, Cameron believed he had the skills to become a commando.

Cameron's grandfather also served in the Australian Army. Here they are together after the March Out Parade which marks the completion of the Army recruit course (courtesy of the Baird family).

Cameron's grandfather and great-grandfather's medals.

Recruits learn many new skills at Kapooka (courtesy of Department of Defence).

DID YOU KNOW?

The ADF was established in 1976 when the Australian government placed the Navy, Army and Air Force under one headquarters. The ADF is responsible for defending Australia, its people and its way of life. The sailors, soldiers and airmen and women also help Australians and people from other countries in times of crisis, such as after a natural disaster.

FAST FACT

In 2016, the Most Outstanding Soldier Award at Kapooka was renamed the Cameron Baird, VC, MG Award.

Chapter 5

EAST TIMOR – KEEPING THE PEACE

Timor is an island that lies to the north of Australia. Its eastern half is a small country called East Timor — Timor-Leste in Tetum, the local language. East Timor is one of the world's newest countries. The people declared independence from the country of Indonesia in 2002. It is also a part of the world that has seen centuries of conflict.

Portuguese traders first arrived in the region of Timor in the 16th century. Portugal later claimed East Timor as a colony, while West Timor became a Dutch colony. During World War II, Japanese forces **invaded** the island of Timor. Australian and Dutch commandos trapped on the island helped civilians to fight the Japanese.

When World War II ended in 1945, Indonesia took control of West Timor, while East Timor remained a Portuguese colony. In 1974, Portugal withdrew and East Timor declared its independence in 1975. Less than two weeks later, Indonesia invaded East Timor and declared it to be part of Indonesia. Over the next twenty years as many as 200,000 East Timorese died resisting the rule of Indonesia. A civil war also broke out. Some East Timorese people wanted their country to remain under the rule of Indonesia. They formed militia groups to fight against people who showed any resistance to the Indonesian forces.

East Timor is one of Australia's closest neighbours. What can you find out about East Timor and its people?

FAST FACT!

The country of East Timor is very small, yet there are many different ethnic groups within the population of approximately 1,300,000 people. Most people are Christian and, while there are 15 different languages spoken, the official languages are Tetum and Portuguese.

In 1999, as Cameron Baird was completing Year 12, the new President of Indonesia announced that the independence of East Timor would be decided by the people. Over 75% of the population voted for independence; they wanted to be their own country under the rule of their own people. The militia groups and some members of the Indonesian military reacted with violence, fighting those who voted for independence.

The United Nations (UN), an international organisation of countries that aims to promote peace, security and cooperation across the world, decided that a **peacekeeping** force was needed to help control the conflict. Servicemen and women from 22 countries combined to help the East Timorese. The force was led by Australia.

Cameron was sent on his first overseas **deployment** to East Timor in April 2001. He was eager to be involved in the peacekeeping mission. Once in the troubled country, he helped to control the militia groups, preventing violence and crime. His tour of duty in East Timor ended in October 2001.

East Timor became an independent **democracy** in 2002 and became known as Timor-Leste. Over the next decade Timor-Leste struggled to become safe and stable. Australian forces, as part of the UN peacekeeping mission, remained there until 2004 but returned two years later when unrest broke out once again. In 2012,the UN ended its peacekeeping mission in Timor-Leste. The last Australian troops left in March 2013.

Although the mission to East Timor lasted many years, Cameron served there only once. There were other places in the world where conflict was brewing in which Cameron's regiment would serve.

FAST FACT!

Indonesia is a country in South-East Asia. It is made up of over 17,000 islands. Indonesia has a population of about 270 million people, most of whom are Muslim belonging to the religion of Islam.

Australian soldiers display their UN Transitional Administration East Timor medals for service in peacekeeping (courtesy Department of Defence).

Australian Peacekeeping Memorial, Canberra, ACT.

Peacekeeping Force

A peacekeeping force is often made up of service personnel from different countries who try to keep the peace between groups or countries in conflict. Australians have been involved in international peacekeeping for more than 70 years.

The United Nations (UN)

The UN was formed in 1945, at the end of World War II. It is an association of countries which aims to promote peace, security and cooperation and helps protect and improve human rights for people all over the world. In 2021 the UN had 193 member nations. In its peacekeeping role the UN invites member countries to help prevent wars. The UN headquarters is in New York in the United States.

The UN provided security for the people of East Timor (courtesy Department of Defence).

An Australian soldier meets some local children in East Timor (courtesy Department of Defence).

General Sir Peter Cosgrove, AK, CVO, MC

General Sir Peter Cosgrove, AK, CVO, MC was in charge of the peacekeeping force in East Timor. He later served as the 26th Governor-General of Australia, from 2014 to 2019.

General Sir Peter Cosgrove, AK, CVO, MC in 2000. He is with a young girl who had been airlifted to Australia for lifesaving medical treatment during the peacekeeping mission in East Timor (courtesy Department of Defence).

An Australian soldier talking to children in East Timor (courtesy Department of Defence).

Tour of Duty

The period of time which service personnel spend in combat or in a hostile environment is known as a tour of duty. During that time, they are on active service, which means they are on duty 24 hours a day, seven days a week.

Chapter 6

AFGHANISTAN – A WAR AGAINST TERRORISM

On 11 September 2001, while Cameron was serving in East Timor, people across the world watched their television screens in horror. Aircraft had been hijacked and flown by **terrorists** into the twin towers of the World Trade Centre in the city of New York in the United States (US). The attacks also saw an aircraft fly into a US government building called the Pentagon. Many people, including Australians, were killed. The terrorist attacks against the US were carried out by an extremist Islamic terrorist group called al-Qaeda. Al-Qaeda was a group of radical followers of Islam from different countries around the world. Osama bin-Laden was the leader of the al-Qaeda terrorists who were based in the country of Afghanistan.

DID YOU KNOW?

Ten Australians were among the 2,977 people who died in the attack on the World Trade Centre in New York. Every year since 2002 a ceremony is held on the anniversary of the attack at which the name of each person is read aloud.

Ground Zero — the site of the World Trade Centre is now a monument to those who lost their lives in the terrorist attack in New York. Photo by Axel Houmadi on Unsplash.

Afghanistan is a country located in central Asia. Its population of 40 million people is made up of many different ethnic groups. Over 50 different languages are spoken. It is a poor country in which wars have been fought for centuries, including wars with Great Britain in the 19th and 20th centuries and civil wars — wars between different groups who live in the same country.

FAST FACT

Afghanistan's full name is The Islamic Republic of Afghanistan. Around 1,500 years ago many of its people followed the Buddhist religion. Islam spread to the region in the 7th century. Today most Afghans are Muslim and follow Islam.

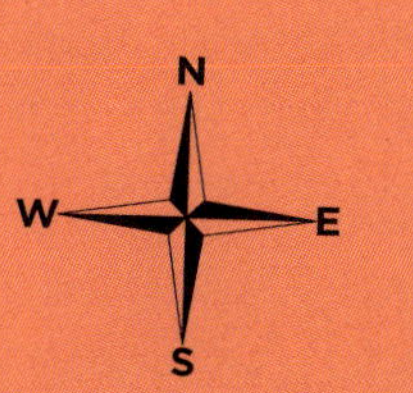

In 1979, Afghanistan was invaded by the Soviet Union. The Soviets remained in the country until 1989. They left behind land mines — bombs which are buried in the ground and can cause terrible injuries when vehicles drive over them or people walk on them. The UN sent an international team, which included some ADF personnel, to help clear the land mines. They returned to Australia in December 1993.

Three years later, an extreme Islamic religious group known as the Taliban took control of Afghanistan. They were supported by the neighbouring country of Pakistan. At first the Taliban were popular because they promised peace, but instead they brought harsh rules and violence. Girls were not allowed to go to school and women were not permitted to work except in some factories, or as nurses and doctors in women's hospitals. Under Taliban rule, family members often taught girls at home, or sent them to secret schools. If caught, the family, teachers and children were severely punished. Many innocent people were killed.

The Taliban had similar views to al-Qaeda and supported the terrorists by welcoming them into Afghanistan, allowing them to recruit and train more followers. Al-Qaeda were opposed to the values of **western nations** and plotted attacks on countries across the world.

After the al-Qaeda attacks in 2001, the US declared a war against terrorism and attacked Afghanistan. Their goal was to capture the leader of al-Qaeda and end the brutal rule of the Taliban. The western nations of Great Britain, Germany, France and Australia supported the US actions and also sent troops. They drove the Taliban from power and helped anti-Taliban forces in Afghanistan to establish a new government. Many terrorists and members of the Taliban fled to Pakistan or into the rugged mountains in rural areas of Afghanistan where they continued to resist the US and its allies.

DID YOU KNOW?

Because it has been at war for so long, the countryside of Afghanistan remains littered with unexploded mines. Children who herd animals are often killed or injured by stepping on these mines. On 16 February 2002, Sergeant Andrew Russell became the first Australian soldier to lose his life in Afghanistan. He was killed when his vehicle drove over a land mine.

Inside a classroom at the Tarin Kowt primary school in Afghanistan. The Australian Army's Reconstruction Task Force later restored the school buildings (courtesy Department of Defence).

DID YOU KNOW?

The Soviet Union, or Union of Soviet Socialist Republics was once the largest country in the world. It was made up of 15 republics, or states, with the Russian republic being the largest and most powerful. The Soviet Union was originally the Russian Empire. In 1917, the tsar, or emperor of the Russian Empire, was removed from power during the Russian Revolution. In 1922, the Soviet Union became the first country in the world to be based on a communist system of government. Under communist rule, individuals do not own their own land or businesses, instead, they belong to the government, or whole community. Any wealth created is supposed to be shared.

Mikhail Gorbachev came to power in 1985, he gave the people more freedom. This eventually led to the 15 republics wanting more independence. In 1991, the Soviet Union came to an end and 15 separate countries were recognised: Russia, Estonia, Latvia, Lithuania, Belarus, Ukraine, Moldova, Georgia, Armenia, Azerbaijan, Kazakhstan, Turkmenistan, Uzbekistan, Tajikistan and Kyrgyzstan.

A Special Operations Task Group engineer conducts training in detecting land mines at Tarin Kowt (courtesy Department of Defence).

Soldiers on patrol in Afghanistan (courtesy Department of Defence).

FAST FACT

Islam is the world's second largest religion with approximately 1.9 billion followers. Christianity is the largest with close to 2.4 billion followers who are called Christians. People who practise Islam are called Muslims.

A Special Operations Task Group engineer conducts training in detecting land mines at Tarin Kowt (courtesy Department of Defence).

FAST FACT

Most followers of Islam are peace-loving people. Islamic terrorist groups have extreme views of their religion. They interpret the teachings of Islam in a radical way to justify their violent actions.

Soon after the attacks on the US, Cameron's tour of duty in East Timor came to an end. Back in Australia, he remained very focused on his training and completed challenging courses, always trying to improve.

In 2002, he achieved his goal of becoming a commando and was awarded the commando green beret. He joined Bravo Company of 2 RAR. Cameron was now well trained to perform the counter-terrorism duties of a commando — working in a team in dangerous situations to search for the enemy and control areas held by terrorists, rescue hostages and protect the rights of innocent people.

It was also in 2002 that innocent people were again attacked by Islamic terrorists. The attack occurred on the Indonesian island of Bali, a popular tourist destination for Australians. Bombs were detonated in and around a nightclub killing 202 people and wounding another 209. Eighty-eight Australians lost their lives. The violent Islamic terrorist group known as Jemaah Islamiyah was responsible. This group had links to al-Qaeda. Osama bin-Laden, the leader of al-Qaeda, declared that the attack was to punish Australia for its support for the war against terrorism and for Australia's role in the liberation of East Timor from the rule of Indonesia.

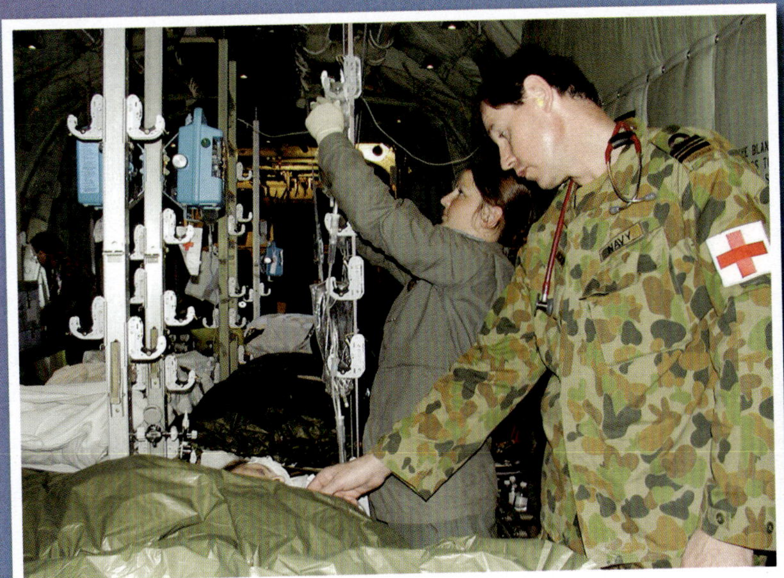

Members of the ADF were sent to Bali to assist those injured in the terrorist attack in 2002 (courtesy Department of Defence).

Chapter 7

IRAQ – THE SECOND GULF WAR 2003–2009

Like Afghanistan, Iraq is a country that has a long history of conflict. It is located in the Middle East, and has a population of over 40 million people which includes many different ethnic groups. It is often called the 'cradle of civilisation' because of the ancient and powerful empires that ruled the region thousands of years ago.

Islam was introduced to Iraq in the 1st century. The city of Baghdad became the world's leading Islamic city. In the 16th century the Ottomans from Turkey conquered Iraq and ruled for almost 400 years. After Turkey was defeated in World War I, Great Britain controlled Iraq until it became an independent country in 1932.

The ruthless dictator Saddam Hussein took control of Iraq in 1979. He ignored the human rights of many citizens. In 1980, after political arguments and disputes about ownership of land and religious differences, he started a long war with the neighbouring country of Iran. Ten years later he invaded the nearby country of Kuwait. Saddam Hussein wanted to control Kuwait's rich oil fields and increase the power of Iraq in the Middle East.

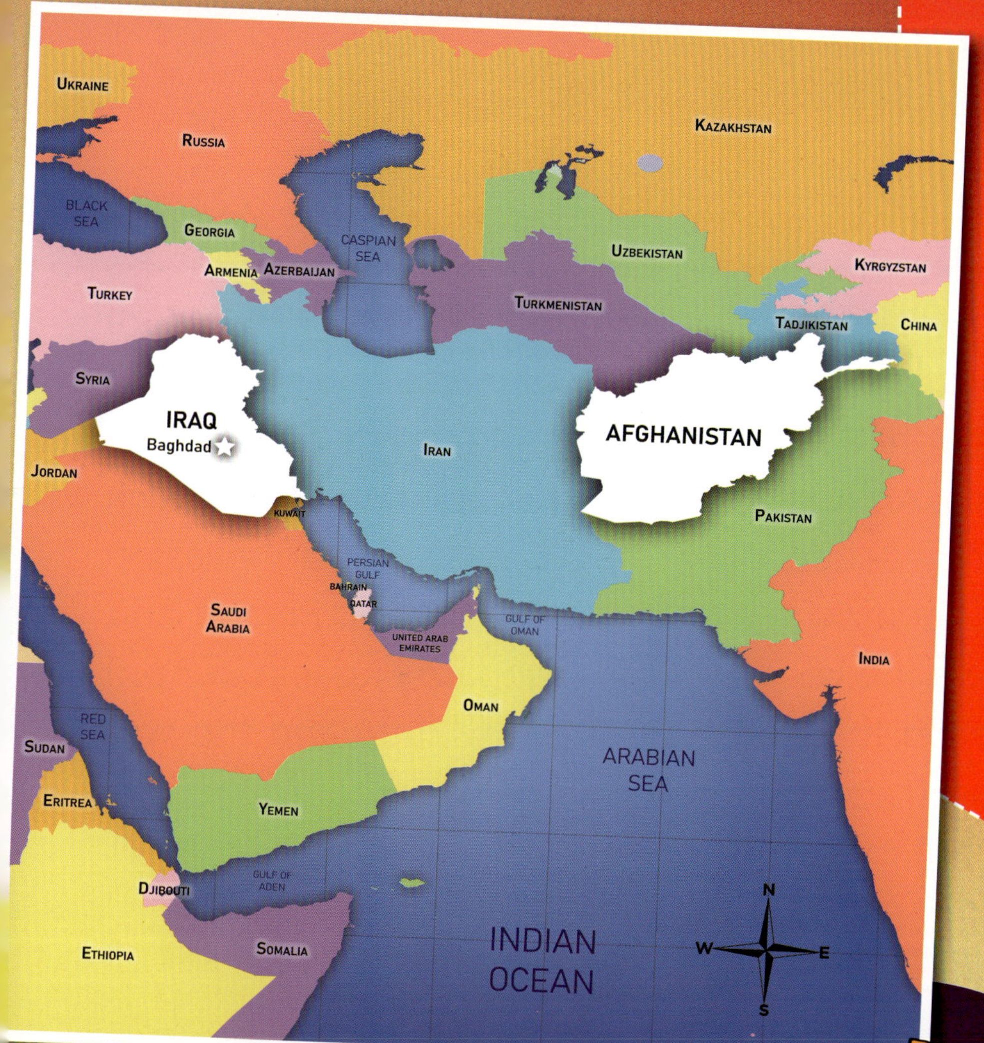

The Middle East

Definitions of which countries and territories make up the Middle East have changed over time. After World War II the following countries were regarded as being in the Middle East: Turkey, Cyprus, Syria, Lebanon, Iraq, Iran, Israel, Palestine (areas within the West Bank and the Gaza Strip), Jordan, Egypt, Sudan, Libya, Saudi Arabia, Kuwait, Yemen, Oman, Bahrain, Qatar, and the United Arab Emirates. Great Britain also has two small territories called Akrotiri and Dhekelia, which are largely military bases on the island of Cyprus.

FAST FACT!

A dictator is a person who takes control of a country and rules with total power, usually without any right to do so and often with force.

The UN raised a force to free Kuwait which included members of the ADF. In April 1991, the country was liberated and the First Gulf War was declared over. Saddam Hussein remained in control of Iraq even though some citizens of Iraq tried to overthrow him.

While fighting the war against terrorism in Afghanistan, the US received information that Saddam Hussein was making dangerous weapons of mass destruction. Such weapons could include bombs and missiles capable of killing large numbers of people and causing great damage to natural and man-made structures. It was thought these weapons could be used to support terrorist groups such as al-Qaeda. Although the UN did not agree to an attack on Iraq, the Australian government supported the US, believing an invasion was needed to support the war against terrorism. Great Britain, Poland and Australia combined forces to help the US overthrow Saddam Hussein in April 2003. This US-led force was called the 'coalition of the willing' and the war was called the Second Gulf War. The chemical weapons were not found and it is now thought that they did not exist.

Australian soldiers from 4 RAR in Iraq in 2003 (courtesy Department of Defence).

Cameron was **deployed** to Iraq with other members of the ADF, including the Navy, Army and Air Force in 2003. He arrived a week after Saddam Hussein had been overthrown. The regiment's role included protecting an airbase from attack by the dictator's supporters until troops from the US arrived.

Cameron landed heavily while exiting from a Hercules aircraft and suffered a painful injury to his back while serving in Iraq. When he returned to Australia the same year, the injury affected his ability to train and perform his duties. Soldiers in the Australian Army agree to serve for a minimum period of two to six years. In his fourth year of service, Cameron chose to leave the Army and return to life as a **civilian**.

Cameron and a fellow soldier in Iraq in 2003 (courtesy of the Baird family).

The United Nations Universal Declaration of Human Rights

In 1948, the UN created an important document which, for the first time, outlined the basic human rights that all people are entitled to, no matter who they are or where they live in the world. The Universal Declaration of Human Rights includes 30 Articles — statements about freedoms and rights which include the right to freedom, to take part in the government of the country, to have a say, practise religion and to humane treatment.

The occupation of Iraq continued while coalition forces searched for weapons and helped to establish a new system of government and a new security force. Most Australian troops returned to Australia in 2009, although some remained in Iraq until 2011 helping to support the new Iraqi government and keeping the country secure from supporters of Saddam Hussein. After the US forces left, a terrorist organisation known as the Islamic State in Iraq and the Levant (ISIL) took over parts of the country. ISIL has since been defeated by the Iraqi government but the country remains in turmoil today.

Cameron with his parents when he returned from Iraq (courtesy of the Baird family).

The Convention on the Rights of the Child

The UN recognised that children needed special protection and in 1989 created The Convention on the Rights of the Child. This is an international agreement outlining the human rights of children. There are 54 articles which can be summarised as all children having the right to:

- Be treated fairly no matter what
- Have a say about decisions affecting them
- Live and grow up healthy
- Have people do what is best for them
- Know who they are and where they come from
- Believe what they want
- Privacy
- Find out information and express their opinion
- Be safe no matter where they are
- Be cared for and have a home
- Education, play and cultural activities
- Help and protection if they need it

Australia has a democratic system of government. What does this mean?

FAST FACT

In January 2005, the Iraqi people voted in the country's first democratic elections in more than 50 years. A National Assembly of representatives were elected to form the Iraqi Transitional Government.

A Seahawk helicopter lands on the deck of HMAS Melbourne in the Persian Gulf in 2003 (courtesy Department of Defence).

The catafalque party rests on arms during the Anzac Day dawn service in Iraq in 2008 (courtesy Department of Defence).

Members of the RAAF in Iraq in 2003 (courtesy Department of Defence).

Chapter 8

OPERATION SLIPPER – AFGHANISTAN

As the Second Gulf War was beginning, life in Afghanistan began to improve under the new government which had been created after the defeat of the Taliban. In May 2003, the US declared that major combat had ended. Some US forces and others from member countries of the North Atlantic Treaty Organisation (NATO) remained to support the government and work with the Afghan people to set up schools, hospitals and public facilities. **Refugees** who had fled the country began to return. Women were free to seek employment and take part in government activities, neither of which were allowed under the Taliban. Thousands of girls, who were previously banned from being educated, were now able to exercise their human right to go to school.

FAST FACT

The North Atlantic Treaty Organisation (NATO) is a military alliance of 28 European countries and two North American countries, the US and Canada. It was formed in 1949 to promote democratic values and protect the security of member countries. The NATO treaty states that an attack on one of the member countries is an attack on all countries.

But the Taliban continued to remain active and gain support in areas outside the Afghan capital, Kabul. Other terrorist groups were also active, such as ISIL, which was opposed to the new government. In some regions of the country the government struggled to keep control.

In 2005, the Australian government agreed to assist by once again deploying troops as part of the Special Operations Task Group to Afghanistan. This commitment was called Operation SLIPPER (Afghanistan). The 1st Reconstruction Task Force was also later deployed to help rebuild important infrastructure like roads and bridges, health care and education facilities. By helping the people of Afghanistan, it was thought they would see that the new Afghan government offered a better life than the Taliban.

The Australians were based at Tarin Kowt in Uruzgan province. Knowing that the war against terrorism was continuing, Cameron decided to rejoin the Army in 2006. He returned to 4 RAR and his role as a commando. In August 2007, at the age of 24, Cameron began the first of four deployments to Afghanistan.

A soldier from the Reconstruction Task Force watches over a causeway worksite in Tarin Kowt in 2007 (courtesy Department of Defence).

Before long, Cameron's leadership qualities were recognised and he was placed in charge of his team of commandos. On his second tour of duty, in a dangerous mission to search for Taliban fighters, fellow commando Luke Worsley was killed in action. A number of civilians also lost their lives. Cameron struggled to cope with the deaths, but his bravery and leadership on the mission helped save the lives of others. Cameron was later awarded the Medal of Gallantry, the third highest award in the Australian military honours system.

Cameron, who was a very humble man, was reluctant to accept the award. He believed his own action was not worthy of an award, but that it had been a team effort and not his alone. Cameron's mates in 4 RAR convinced him that the individual honour was an honour for the entire regiment.

Australian soldiers hand out soccer balls donated by Brisbane boy Mac Millar to children at a boys' school in Uruzgan province, Afghanistan (courtesy Department of Defence).

HMAS *Darwin* patrolling in the Middle East to promote security in the area and deter terrorism. Crew members in inflatable boats are approaching a suspicious vessel (courtesy Department of Defence).

To Gallipoli

Cameron returned to Australia in January 2008. He was then chosen as one of 15 Australian soldiers to promote the values of the Australian Army to other soldiers in a program known as 'I'm an Australian Soldier'.

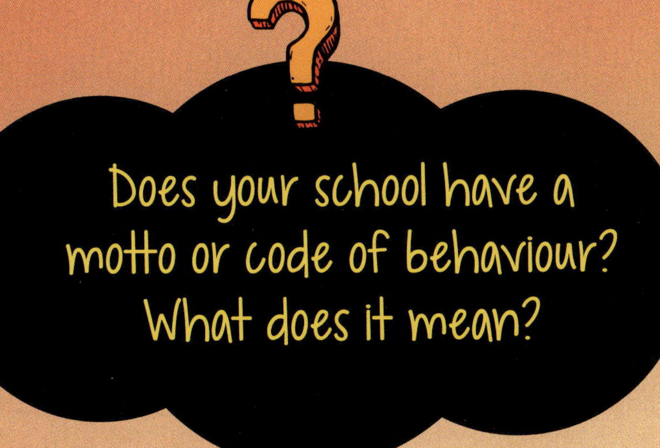

The Values of the Australian Defence Force

Service
Courage
Respect
Integrity
Excellence

The program involved learning about the Gallipoli **campaign** in World War I and the actions of the first Anzacs — the soldiers of the Australian and New Zealand Army **Corps** who landed at Anzac Cove on the Gallipoli peninsula in Turkey on 25 April 1915. Cameron was mentored by Major John Thurgar who had served in the Vietnam War. Major Thurgar was impressed by Cameron's attitude and skills.

The Army's Contract with Australia

I'm an Australian soldier who is an expert in close combat
I am physically and mentally tough
compassionate and courageous
I lead by example, I strive to take the initiative
I am committed to learning and working for the team
I believe in trust, loyalty and respect
for my country, my mates and the Army
the Rising Sun is my badge of honour
I am an Australian Soldier – always

The earliest known photograph of troops landing at Anzac Cove, taken at around 5.30 am on 25 April 1915 (AWM P10140.004).

He was just honest and reliable and trustworthy … all the qualities you'd want in a soldier and a best mate.

Major John Thurgar, SASR

An Anzac Day service at Lone Pine, Gallipoli, 2019 (courtesy Department of Defence).

At Gallipoli, Cameron was billeted with a Turkish family who helped him understand Islam as practised by most Muslims — not the extreme and radical practices of the Taliban, al-Qaeda or ISIL. The 15 soldiers also connected with their Anzac forebears. They paddled in kayaks to Anzac Cove, reliving the pre-dawn experience of the first Anzacs who landed at Gallipoli in 1915. They also visited the graves of those who lost their lives.

Cameron was inspired to work even harder to become the best soldier possible.

The Anzac Spirit — character strengths

The Anzac spirit refers to a set of character strengths. It is a legacy which has become an important part of our national identity. The original Anzacs displayed courage, mateship, resourcefulness, endurance and sacrifice. Many people believe these qualities have helped to form our traditions, our culture and our ideas on what it means to be an Australian.

Can you recognise the qualities of the Anzac spirit in Cameron Baird?

What does the Anzac spirit mean to you and your family?

Do you see people displaying the qualities of the Anzac spirit today?

Anzac stood, and still stands for reckless valour in a good cause, for enterprise, resourcefulness, fidelity, comradeship and endurance that will never own defeat.

C.E.W. Bean (1946)

Cameron at home in 2008 (courtesy of the Baird family).

DID YOU KNOW?

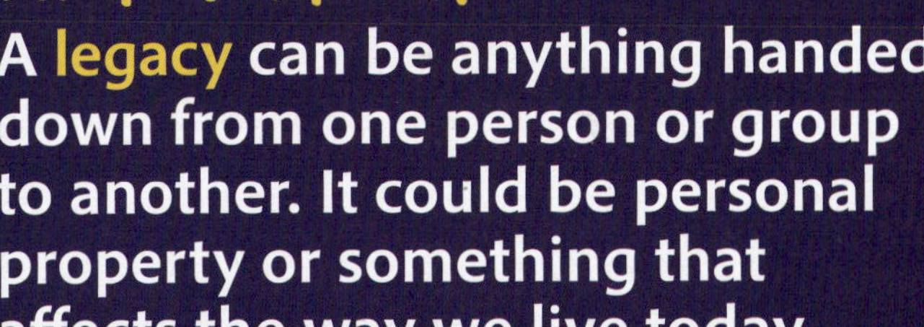

A **legacy** can be anything handed down from one person or group to another. It could be personal property or something that affects the way we live today.

A Lasting Legacy

Cameron left a lasting legacy in his interaction with family members, friends, his peers and generally anyone who had the opportunity to meet him. Cam Baird, or 'Bairdy' as he was known, was simply the most extraordinary person we have had the pleasure to meet, teach and call a mate. All who knew Cam will attest to his intelligence, ingenuity, kindness, sense of humility, courage, inclusiveness and leadership. He lived his life guided by a strong set of values.

Cameron's friend Chris Dyer and teacher Andrew Harrison

The Catafalque Party presents arms during an Anzac Day service at Lone Pine, Gallipoli.

DID YOU KNOW?

Many international organisations worked in Afghanistan to help provide the basic human rights of safety, food and shelter. The Red Cross or Red Crescent, as it is called in Muslim countries, helps refugees find family members (a cross is a symbol of Christianity and a crescent is a symbol of Islam). The United Nations Children's Fund and Save the Children sponsor education while other organisations help rebuild schools, hospitals and roads.

FAST FACT

In 2017 the UN estimated that one-third of Afghanistan's population needed aid. Although governments have provided money to help rebuild the country, many people still live in poverty.

Children drink water from a pump outside their house in Tarin Kowt, Afghanistan (courtesy Department of Defence).

Students at an Australian-funded boys' school in Uruzgan province, Afghanistan (courtesy Department of Defence).

DID YOU KNOW?

The United Nations Convention on the Rights of the Child states that all children have the right to a good-quality education and should be encouraged to achieve the highest level of education possible. Cameron Baird believed in this basic right and would frequently encourage younger people to try hard at school. Under the rule of the Taliban, millions of children are not permitted to go to school.

FAST FACT

An insurgent is someone who uses violence to fight against the lawful government. Members of the Taliban are insurgents who fought against the government of Afghanistan.

Corporal Cameron Baird, VC, MG (second from right) with members of his team in Afghanistan in 2011 (courtesy Department of Defence).

In July 2009, 4 RAR was renamed the 2nd Commando Regiment. That year Cameron completed his second tour of duty to Afghanistan. Two years later, he returned to the troubled country. Australian troops were now involved in mentoring troops from the Afghan forces, teaching them valuable soldiering skills to prepare for when the government of Afghanistan could take control without the support of other countries. Australians had been training the Afghan National Army since 2008. This tour of eight months was to be the longest Cameron had experienced in Afghanistan. He spent his free time reading books and building understanding and rapport with the Afghan troops by interacting with them socially.

Members of the Special Operations Task Group cross the harsh terrain between mountains in Uruzgan province in the winter of 2011 (courtesy Department of Defence).

A soldier of the 2nd Cavalry Regiment Task Force chats to local children during a patrol through Tarin Kowt, Afghanistan (courtesy Department of Defence).

In 2013, Cameron returned to Afghanistan on his fourth tour of duty. He knew it was likely to be his last as he would soon be promoted to the rank of sergeant. As an exemplary leader and with his experience, Cameron's excellent skills and ability to mentor and lead others could be used to train other commandos. But there was more work to be done in Afghanistan, including preparing Afghan troops to take control of their country.

Corporal Cameron Baird, VC, MG in Afghanistan in 2013 (courtesy Department of Defence).

Corporal Cameron Baird, VC, MG in Afghanistan in 2013 (courtesy Department of Defence).

In June, Cameron was involved in a dangerous mission to clear a village of Taliban insurgents. The commandos reached the village of Ghawchak in Uruzgan province by helicopter. Soon after, they came under fire from Taliban forces. Throughout the morning they battled to win control of the village.

Cameron was commanding his team when a call came through his communication system. A mate, the leader of another team some distance away, had been seriously wounded. The team was under heavy fire. Cameron made the immediate decision to lead his team to assist. Despite the risks to his own safety from Taliban fighters firing machine-guns, Cameron continued his mission to rescue his fellow soldier.

Cameron led his team into the building from which the Taliban fighters were firing their weapons. Showing great courage, he charged the enemy three times to draw their fire away from his team so they could reach the wounded soldier.

He was killed on his third attempt.

Corporal Cameron Baird, VC, MG in Afghanistan in 2013 (courtesy Department of Defence).

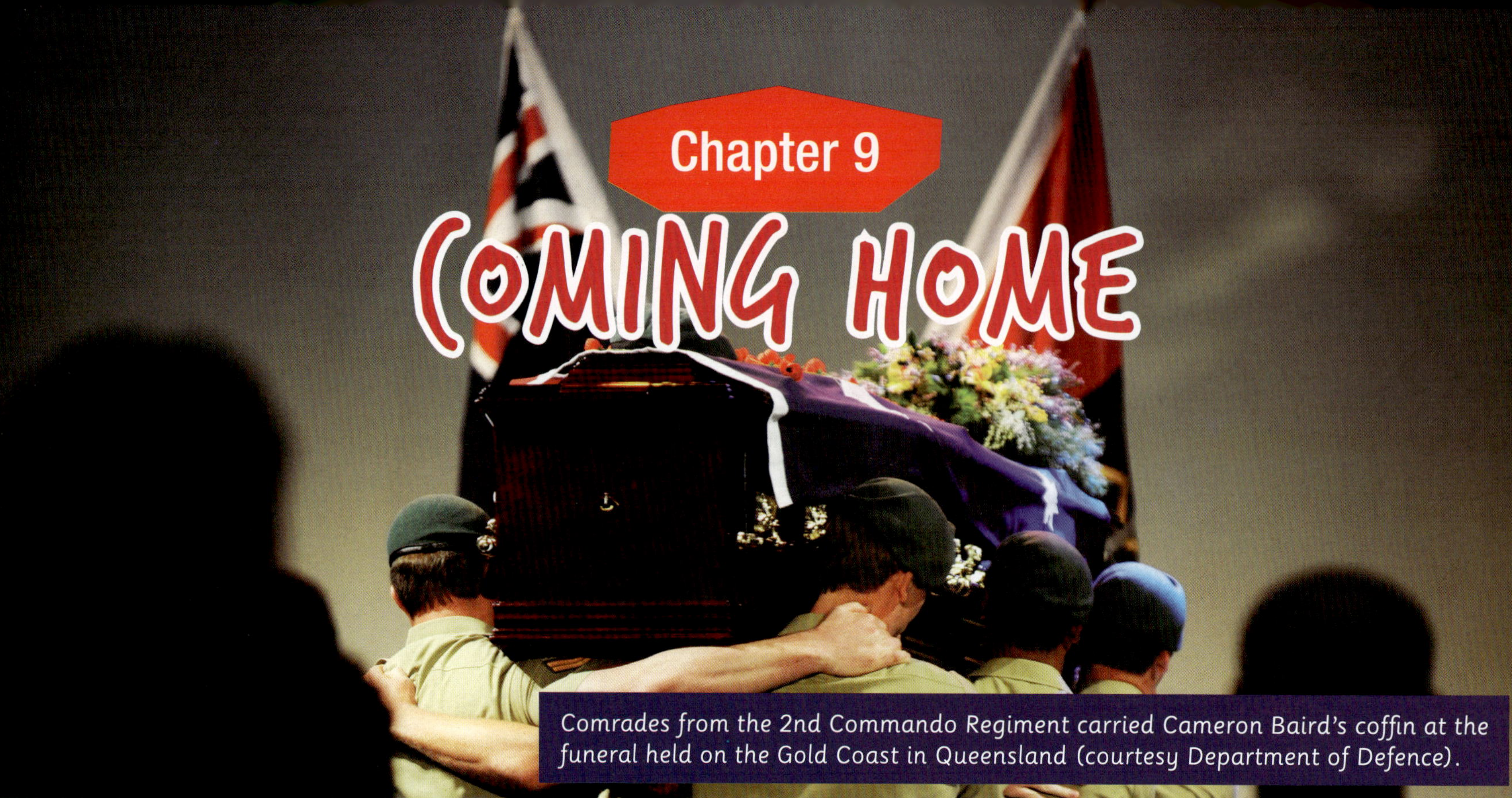

Chapter 9

Coming Home

Comrades from the 2nd Commando Regiment carried Cameron Baird's coffin at the funeral held on the Gold Coast in Queensland (courtesy Department of Defence).

Just a few minutes passed between the time when the call arrived with news of his wounded mate and the moment of Cameron's death. In that brief period, his actions and those of his team saved the lives of others. Cameron's mate was rescued and survived his wounds. Both teams returned safely to Tarin Kowt. But they had lost an outstanding Australian soldier.

ADF personnel at Tarin Kowt formed up to pay their respects to Cameron in a moving **ramp ceremony** as he began the first leg of his journey back to Australia. They were farewelling a soldier they had respected and trusted — a courageous and admired leader who always looked out for his teammates. Inside Cameron's locker were found the words 'Aspire to Inspire' along with a folder with images and information on the other Australians who had died in Afghanistan. These men were his inspiration.

Another ceremony was held when the aircraft carrying his body landed at RAAF Base Richmond, in New South Wales, where Cameron's family waited.

Cameron is buried on the Gold Coast in Queensland close to where his parents live today.

In combat and as a team commander, he was the man to watch and was never happier than when the situation demanded decisive action and courage. He was described by colleagues as one of the most iconic figures in the regiment. Corporal Baird was a modern-day warrior who set a standard that every soldier aspires to achieve.

General David Hurley, then Chief of Defence, now Governor-General of Australia (courtesy of the Baird family).

Cameron was farewelled from Tarin Kowt in a solemn service of remembrance and ramp ceremony (courtesy Department of Defence).

Soldiers from the 2nd Commando Regiment form a catafalque party surrounding Cameron's coffin at the service of remembrance and ramp ceremony at Tarin Kowt (courtesy Department of Defence).

Cam Baird is and will always be one of the most inspiring leaders within the 2nd Commando Regiment. There is not one of us who would not follow him into any combat situation. His moral, physical and mental standards provided a guiding light for each of us to follow. He will never be forgotten.

Major P, Cameron's Commanding Officer (courtesy of the Baird family).

Army Regimental Sergeant-Major Warrant Officer David Ashley said that he did not know of any other soldier who was so highly regarded. I know that Cameron Baird is one of Australia's greatest ever soldiers (courtesy of the Baird family).

Cameron's grave

Chapter 10

VICTORIA CROSS

Six months after that fateful day in Afghanistan, the Australian Prime Minister announced in parliament that Cameron had been awarded Australia's 100th Victoria Cross for his actions on 22 June 2013.

The Victoria Cross for Australia is the country's highest award for valour. It is awarded for conspicuous gallantry, acts of valour or self-sacrifice, or displays of extreme devotion to duty in the face of the enemy. The original Victoria Cross was created in 1856 during the reign of Great Britain's Queen Victoria.

In 1975, Australia developed its own system of awards and honours to replace the British system. The Victoria Cross was renamed the Victoria Cross for Australia and ratified by Queen Elizabeth II in 1991. It is the same design and its awarding must be approved by the Queen. Since 1856, there have been 101 Victoria Crosses awarded to Australians. Of the five Australians who have been awarded the Victoria Cross for Australia since 1991, two have received the award posthumously. This means they received the medal after they died.

Part of the citation for Cameron's Victoria Cross reads:

For the most conspicuous acts of valour, extreme devotion to duty and ultimate self-sacrifice at Ghawchak village, Uruzgan province, Afghanistan, as a Commando Team Commander in Special Operations Task Group on Operation SLIPPER ... Corporal Baird's acts of valour and self-sacrifice regained the initiative and preserved the lives of his team members. His actions were of the highest order and in keeping with the finest traditions of the Australian Army and the Australian Defence Force.

Cameron's medals are on display at the Australian War Memorial in Canberra (courtesy Department of Defence).

The medal was presented to Cameron's parents and brother by Australia's Governor-General at the time, The Honourable Quentin Bryce, AD, CVO. Cameron's parents held the medal forward and pointed it towards the members of the 2nd Commando Regiment who were present. They knew Cameron would want to acknowledge his team.

The Governor-General, Her Excellency The Honourable Quentin Bryce, AC, CVO, presented the Victoria Cross for Australia to Cameron's parents (courtesy Department of Defence).

Cameron's family in 2014 at the service for the award of the Victoria Cross for Australia at Parliament House, Canberra (courtesy Department of Defence).

FAST FACT!

Created in 1856 during the reign of Queen Victoria, the Victoria Cross has a crimson ribbon and a bronze Maltese Cross. The bronze comes from a Russian cannon which was captured by the British in the Crimean War.

Medals and Honours

For centuries, kings, queens and governments have rewarded units and individuals for outstanding service. Members of the ADF are awarded medals for their service during times of conflict, or outstanding service when not at war. They can also receive medals which honour acts of bravery or leadership in battle. Coloured ribbons are attached to the medal and there are rules about the order in which the medals are positioned. Servicemen and women wear their own medals on their left side over their heart.

Australian Gallantry Decorations

Gallantry decorations are awarded for acts of bravery in warlike conditions which are beyond those normally expected of people in similar situations. They can only be awarded to members of the ADF.

The Australian gallantry decorations are (starting with the highest):

- Victoria Cross for Australia
- Star of Gallantry
- Medal for Gallantry
- Commendation for Gallantry

Trooper Mark Donaldson who also served in Afghanistan was awarded the first Victoria Cross for Australia since it was renamed in 1991 (courtesy Department of Defence).

Australia's First Victoria Cross Recipient — Major General Sir Neville Reginald Howse, VC, KCB, KCMG, FRCS

Neville Howse was the first Australian to be awarded the Victoria Cross. He served in the Boer War which took place in South Africa from 1899 to 1902. It was a war between British and Commonwealth Forces on one side and the Dutch South Africans, known as the Boers, on the other. The war was sparked by the discovery of gold and diamonds in parts of southern Africa, lands which both the British and Dutch had colonised in the 1600s and 1700s. An Army captain at the time, Howse was a doctor who rescued a wounded soldier while under enemy fire. He later operated on the soldier and saved the man's life. He also served in World War I and was involved in the evacuation of wounded soldiers from Gallipoli.

Ordinary Seaman Edward (Teddy) Sheean, RAN (AWM 044154)

DID YOU KNOW?

The coloured stripes of ribbons attached to medals show the campaign for which the medal was awarded and which services were involved in that campaign. Usually a navy-blue stripe represents the Navy, the Army stripe is red and the RAAF is light blue. Other colours on the ribbon show where the campaign was located e.g. a jungle might be green, the desert a sand colour, or the ocean might be blue.

The 101st Victoria Cross for Australia — Ordinary Seaman Edward 'Teddy' Sheean, VC

Eighteen-year-old Teddy Sheean, VC is the most recent recipient of the Victoria Cross for Australia and the first member of the RAN to receive the award. Teddy was on board HMAS *Armidale* when it was attacked on 1 November 1942 by Japanese aircraft during World War II.

Teddy was Mentioned in Despatches for his bravery but was not awarded the Victoria Cross at the time. Family and community members continued to fight for recognition of Teddy's courage and an expert panel was formed to review his actions. On 1 December 2020, exactly 78 years after the sinking of the ship and Teddy's death, the Governor-General presented the Victoria Cross of Australia to Teddy's family.

An Anzac Day dawn service, Greenwell Point, New South Wales, 2019 (courtesy Department of Defence).

FAST FACT!

People who have served in the armed forces are called veterans.

While serving in the Australian Army, Cameron was deployed on the following operations:

- Operation TANAGER (Timor-Leste) — April–October 2001
- Operation BASTILLE (Iraq) — February–March 2003
- Operation FALCONER (Iraq) — March–May 2003
- Operation SLIPPER (Afghanistan) — August 2007–January 2008
- Operation SLIPPER (Afghanistan) — March–July 2009
- Operation SLIPPER (Afghanistan) — July 2011–February 2012
- Operation SLIPPER (Afghanistan) — February–June 2013

Corporal Cameron Baird was awarded the following honours and awards for his service:

- Victoria Cross for Australia
- Medal for Gallantry
- Australian Active Service Medal with East Timor, Iraq 2003 and International Coalition against Terrorism clasps
- Afghanistan Medal
- Iraq Medal
- Australian Service Medal with Counter Terrorism/Special Recovery clasps
- Australian Defence Medal
- United Nations Medal with Ribbon United Nations Transitional Authority in East Timor
- NATO Meritorious Service Medal
- NATO Non-Article 5 Medal with International Security Assistance Force and multi-tour indicator 3
- Meritorious Unit Citation - Task Force 66 (Special Operations Task Group), Afghanistan
- Infantry Combat Badge
- Returned from Active Service Badge.

Why are awards and medals presented to service personnel?

Why do people choose to wear an ancestor's medals on Anzac Day and Remembrance Day?

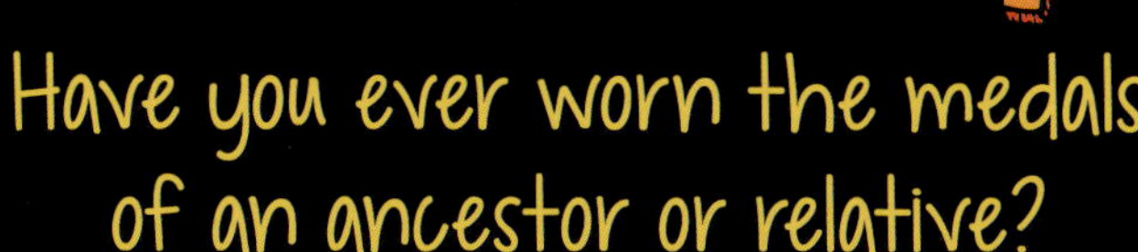

Have you ever worn the medals of an ancestor or relative?

The NATO Meritorious Service Medal awarded to Corporal Cameron Baird, VC, MG (courtesy Department of Defence).

Chapter 11

AFGHANISTAN – 2021

Operation SLIPPER began in 2002 and concluded in 2013. During this time, attendance at Afghan schools increased, particularly by girls, there was less violence and crime, and women could once again go to work. But the securing of these basic human rights was not achieved without casualties and great sacrifice from all the nations involved. Forty-one Australian soldiers were killed and 259 wounded.

Even after the end of Operation Slipper on 15 December 2013, ADF personnel and military staff from other countries remained in Afghanistan to help advise and train the Afghan National Army to build defence and counter-terrorism forces.

Graduates of the trade training school proudly display their certificates and toolkits after their graduation ceremony at Multi-National Base - Tarin Kowt in 2013 (courtesy Department of Defence).

Evacuees from Afghanistan board a flight to Australia from the ADF's main operating base in the Middle East. They had earlier been evacuated from Kabul (courtesy of Department of Defence).

The Afghanistan Memorial, Canberra, ACT.

In 2020, the Taliban and the Afghan government began to discuss a peace treaty. In November 2020 the US President, Donald Trump, ordered his forces to begin withdrawing from Afghanistan. Later, the new US President, Joe Biden, announced that he planned to withdraw his troops from Afghanistan by May 2021. The withdrawal date was later extended to 31 August 2021.

On 14 April 2021, NATO began to withdraw troops and staff. At that time there were approximately 9,500 personnel from 36 countries working with the NATO force, including 80 Australians.

As international troops began to withdraw, the Taliban resumed its battle to rule Afghanistan, occupying several cities and reintroducing its extreme views and disregard for human rights. By 15 August 2021, the Taliban had taken control of all major cities, including the capital, Kabul. President Ashraf Ghani fled the country, and the Afghan government collapsed. The Taliban had regained power.

Countries sent aircraft to rescue supporters of the Afghan government and foreign personnel who had remained. Australia deployed five aircraft and a team from the Army to evacuate Australians and approved people who were not Australian citizens from Kabul.

After nearly 20 years in Afghanistan, Australia's longest war had ended.

Supreme Sacrifice

Forty-one Australian soldiers were killed in Afghanistan (34 as a result of enemy action) and 261 wounded (including two sailors and one airman). They were the first Australian deaths in combat since the Vietnam War.

Sergeant Andrew Russell, 33
Trooper David Pearce, 41
Sergeant Matthew Locke, MG, 33
Private Luke Worsley, 26
Lance Corporal Jason Marks, 27
Signalman Sean McCarthy, 25
Lieutenant Michael Fussell, 25
Private Gregory Michael Sher, 30
Corporal Mathew Hopkins, 21
Sergeant Brett Till, 31
Private Benjamin Ranaudo, 22
Sapper Jacob Moerland, 21
Sapper Darren Smith, 25
Private Scott Palmer, 27
Private Timothy Aplin, 38
Private Benjamin Chuck, 27
Private Nathan Bewes, 23
Trooper Jason Brown, 29
Private Grant Kirby, 35
Private Tomas Dale, 21
Lance Corporal Jared MacKinney, 28
Corporal Richard Atkinson, 22
Sapper Jamie Larcombe, 21
Sergeant Brett Wood, MG, DSM, 32
Lance Corporal Andrew Jones, 25
Lieutenant Marcus Sean Case, 27
Sapper Rowan Robinson, 23
Sergeant Todd Langley, 35
Private Matthew Lambert, 26
Captain Bryce Duffy, 26
Corporal Ashley Birt, 22
Lance Corporal Luke Gavin, 27
Sergeant Blaine Diddams, MG, 40
Private Nathanael John Aubrey Galagher, 23
Lance Corporal Mervyn John McDonald, 30
Lance Corporal Stjepan Milosevic, 40
Private Robert Hugh Frederick Poate, 23
Sapper James Thomas Martin, 21
Corporal Scott James Smith, 24
Corporal Cameron Stewart Baird, VC, MG, 32
Lance Corporal Todd John Chidgey, 29

Another Australian, Rifleman Stuart Nash, was killed while serving with the British Army

2 COM
APLIN T. J.
BAIRD C. S.
UCK B. A.
GALAGHER N. J.
6

Chapter 12

Remembering Corporal Cameron Baird, VC, MG

Serving in conflict zones is challenging and veterans often need support to overcome not only physical injuries but also the impact of trauma known as Post Traumatic Stress Disorder. Families who have lost loved ones or who care for those with injuries also need support. After Cameron's death, his parents dedicated their time to helping raise money and awareness for charities which support veterans and their families.

In 2014, with the support of Cameron's parents, his schoolfriend Chris Dyer and his former teacher and first footy coach Andrew Harrison, created a charity called Cam's Cause to raise funds for veterans. Later, Cameron's other schoolmates, Daniel Carroll and Rick Green, also became involved. They regard it as Cameron's legacy. Cam's Cause honours Cameron's qualities and spirit, increases knowledge and understanding of the war in Afghanistan and, as Cameron would want — it helps his mates.

Cameron's motto was ***Aspire to Inspire***. He was always striving to do the best he could. After Cameron passed away, a young student named Campbell Byrd contacted the Baird family. Campbell had written to an unknown soldier as part of a class project. Cameron received the student's letter and replied in May 2013:

Sometimes my job is difficult but I have good reasons to do it. Making the world a safer place for others is one reason. I think we are very lucky in Australia, we are safe and can live our lives as we wish …

Always try your best in whatever you do, and always be happy in your life.

Australian Army soldier Corporal Cameron Baird, VC, MG (Courtesy Department of Defence).

There are many ways in which people commemorate others who have served their country in times of conflict. Across Australia and the world, Cameron's inspirational commitment, courage, loyalty and his selfless actions are remembered in memorials ranging from monuments and statues, the naming of a military base and sporting awards, to poetry, portraits and books. Each one of these tributes reminds us to be grateful for his service and sacrifice, and that of all Australian servicemen and women.

Soldiers from the 2nd Commando Regiment escort Cameron's parents and his brother to the Pool of Reflection to lay a wreath commemorating Corporal Cameron Baird, VC, MG, during the Last Post Ceremony at the Australian War Memorial, Canberra, in his honour on 13 May 2015 (courtesy Department of Defence).

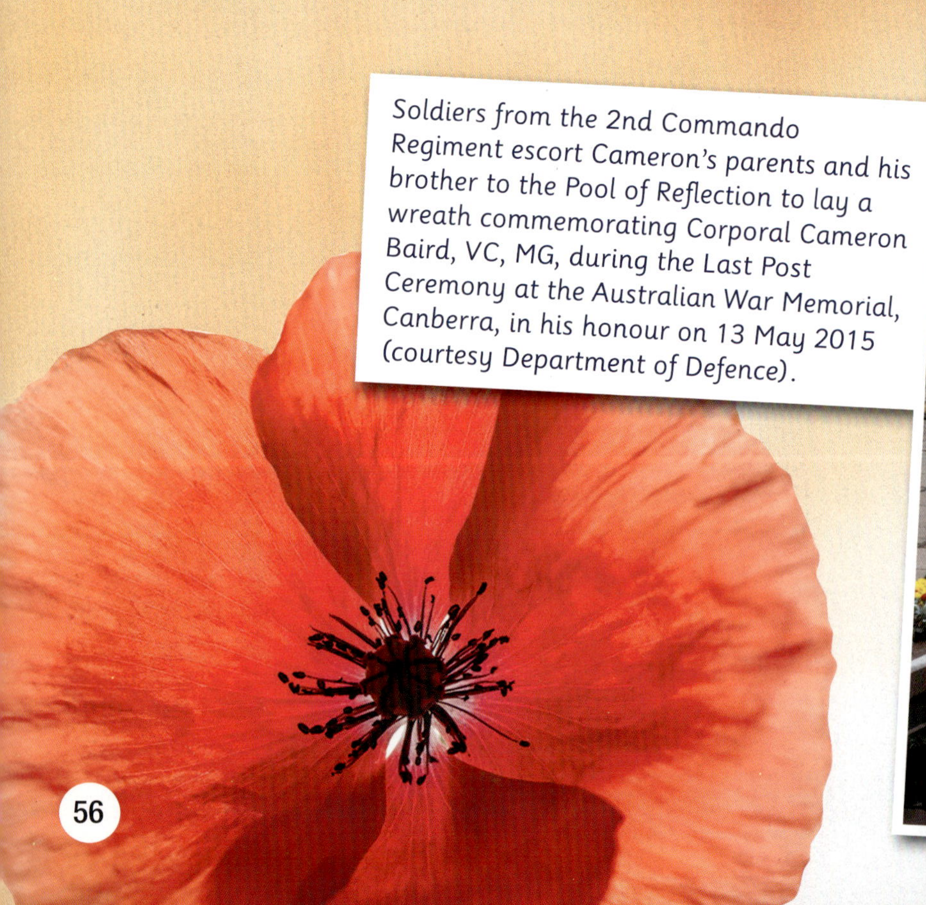

Artist George Petrou's painting of Corporal Baird at the Australian National Veterans Art Museum in Melbourne (courtesy George Petrou).

Chapter 13

ACTIVITIES

Commemoration with Poetry

People commemorate or honour the memory of an event, a group of people or a person in many different ways. This is an excerpt from a poem written in 2015 about Corporal Cameron Baird, VC, MG. It was written by former soldier Corporal Elena Rowland.

Can you construct your own commemorative poem about Cameron or someone you know, perhaps an ancestor or a relative? Try using words found in this book such as leadership, commitment, courage, bravery, spirit, valour, legacy and sacrifice.

The Australian government renamed the ADF's forward operating air base at Al Minhad, near Dubai in the United Arab Emirates, Camp Baird in Cameron's honour (courtesy Department of Defence).

Burnie Boy

Just a Tassie boy from Burnie town
with a smile as big as a moon,
made his mum and dad so proud
that day he came in June.
Born for a purpose and a destined path
this little boy grew big.
With seasons that pushed towards his fate,
young Cam became a dig.
With a humble heart and determined will,
success became his prey.
The commando in him exploded out,
a legend was born that day.
With spirit and honour Cam went to war,
over and over again,
his courage shone and inspired all ...

A fearless leader, he led from the front ...
Cam charged towards the foe ...

This was the plan, God had all along,
To teach us how we should live.
Not to take but how we should give.
So rest in peace young Burnie boy,
Your legacy will remain.
For the debt you paid, we'll never forget,
for it fuels the eternal flame.

Excerpt from 'Burnie Boy' by Corporal Elena Rowland (courtesy of the Baird family).

Make a Family or Class Medal of Courage

Look at the Victoria Cross medal. What is valour?

Copy the template below.

What colours will you choose for the ribbon?

What symbols will you use?

Design a Commemorative Stamp

Postage stamps are often designed to commemorate people and events. Australia Post created an Australian Legends stamp series in which Corporal Cameron Baird was included.

Design a stamp to honour an Australian serviceman or woman you admire, or create a design to commemorate Anzac Day or Remembrance Day.

GLOSSARY

Australian Imperial Force (AIF) - the volunteer Australian military force that served overseas in World War I. In World War II it was known as the 2nd AIF.

Campaign - military plans and combat actions aiming to resolve a conflict.

Conflict - disagreements between people or groups such as a struggle for power or property.

Civilian - A person who does not belong to the armed forces.

Corps - a combined army unit or group. It is pronounced 'core'.

Democracy - a form of government in which the power is held by the people, usually through elected representatives.

Democratic - where decisions are made by leaders elected by others.

Deployed/deployment - moving military personnel and materials from a home base to another destination.

Ethnic - part of a nation, race or people with shared cultural traditions.

Invade - enter a place with military forces to take it over.

Land mine - a bomb which is on, or under the ground which explodes when walked on or driven over.

Memorial - something designed to honour an event, group of people or a person who has died.

Mourning - to grieve for someone who has died, or for the loss of something valued.

Peacekeeping - armed forces keeping the peace between groups or countries in conflict.

Ramp ceremony - a memorial service for a fallen soldier, held at the airport prior to the departure of the aircraft carrying the body, or for the arrival of the same aircraft at the soldier's home base.

Refugee - a person forced to leave his or her country or home because it is not safe to remain, often in time of war or during a natural disaster.

Regiment - a military unit of ground force soldiers.

Servicemen and women - men and women who serve in the armed forces.

Terrorist - a person who uses violence against people and places to force a government to change.

Unit - an individual group of soldiers who make up a larger group.

INDEX

BIBLIOGRAPHY

Australian Army History Unit, *A Brief History of the Australian Army*, Big Sky Publishing, Newport, NSW, 2017.

McKelvey, Ben, *The Commando: the Life and Death of Cameron Baird, VC, MG*, Hachette, Australia, 2017.

Paterson, Allison, *Australia Remembers: Anzac Day, Remembrance Day and War Memorials*, Big Sky Publishing, Newport, NSW, 2018.

Paterson, Allison, *Australia Remembers 2: Customs and Traditions of the Australian Defence Force*, Big Sky Publishing, Newport, NSW, 2021.

Petrou, George, *The Art of Sacrifice*, Big Sky Publishing, Newport, NSW, 2021.

Websites:

Australian Army: www.army.gov.au

Australian Defence Force: www.defence.gov.au

Australian War Memorial: www.awm.gov.au

Acknowledgements

First and foremost, I extend my gratitude to Cameron's parents, Doug and Kaye Baird — thank you for trusting me with your son's story, welcoming me into your home, and for your advice and thoughts throughout. Thanks also to Cameron's friend Chris Dyer and teacher Andrew Harrison for their assistance and words.

My thanks also to Ben McKelvey, author of *The Commando: the Life and Death of Cameron Baird*, which describes Cameron's childhood and his experiences serving with the Australian Army. My gratitude also to artist George Petrou for first introducing me to Cameron's story while we worked together on the creation of his wonderful book *The Art of Sacrifice*.

Thank you to my husband Rob Paterson, who not only takes great photos, but offers constant encouragement, support and honest comment, as do all the family! To my beta-readers, Rob Paterson and Lyn Rees, my sincere gratitude. Also to the Brand Managers and Digital Media Team of the Australian Defence Force and Army for their assistance and advice.

I would like to offer my endless appreciation to Denny Neave, Sharon Evans and Diane Evans at Big Sky Publishing, along with their talented design team, Pat Kan and Chris Nesci. Your dedication to the preservation of Australia's history is inspirational. Much gratitude also to Cathy McCullagh, a very forgiving and patient editor whose experience, skill and insight are greatly respected and valued, as is her friendship.

ABOUT THE AUTHOR

Allison Paterson is the author of the 2016 ABIA and CBCA-longlisted title *Anzac Sons: Five Brothers on the Western Front*, the children's version of the adult non-fiction title *Anzac Sons: the Story of Five Brothers in the War to End All Wars*. Both are based on a collection of over 500 letters sent from the Western Front by her grandfather and his four brothers. Her children's picture books, *Granny's Place* and *Shearing Time*, are inspired by childhood memories of her grandparents and life on the farm. *Australia Remembers: Anzac Day, Remembrance Day and War Memorials* is the first volume in the Australia Remembers series and was published in 2018. *Australia Remembers: Customs and Traditions of the Australian Defence Force* followed soon after.

In 2021 Allison released a picture book about marine pollution and sustainability called *I Wonder* and followed that with a picture book created in partnership with volunteer organisation Children's Rights Queensland. The book about children's rights is titled *The Right to Be Me*. Allison was a teacher-librarian for over 20 years and has reviewed children's literature for *Magpies Magazine* for almost as long. She was a recipient of a 2017 May Gibbs Children's Literature Trust Creative Time Fellowship. The resulting young adult manuscript *Follow After Me* was released in 2019. Allison now works as a writer, presenter and publishing consultant.

If you would like to invite Allison to visit your school, you can contact her at:
www.allisonmarlowpaterson.com

Available September 2022

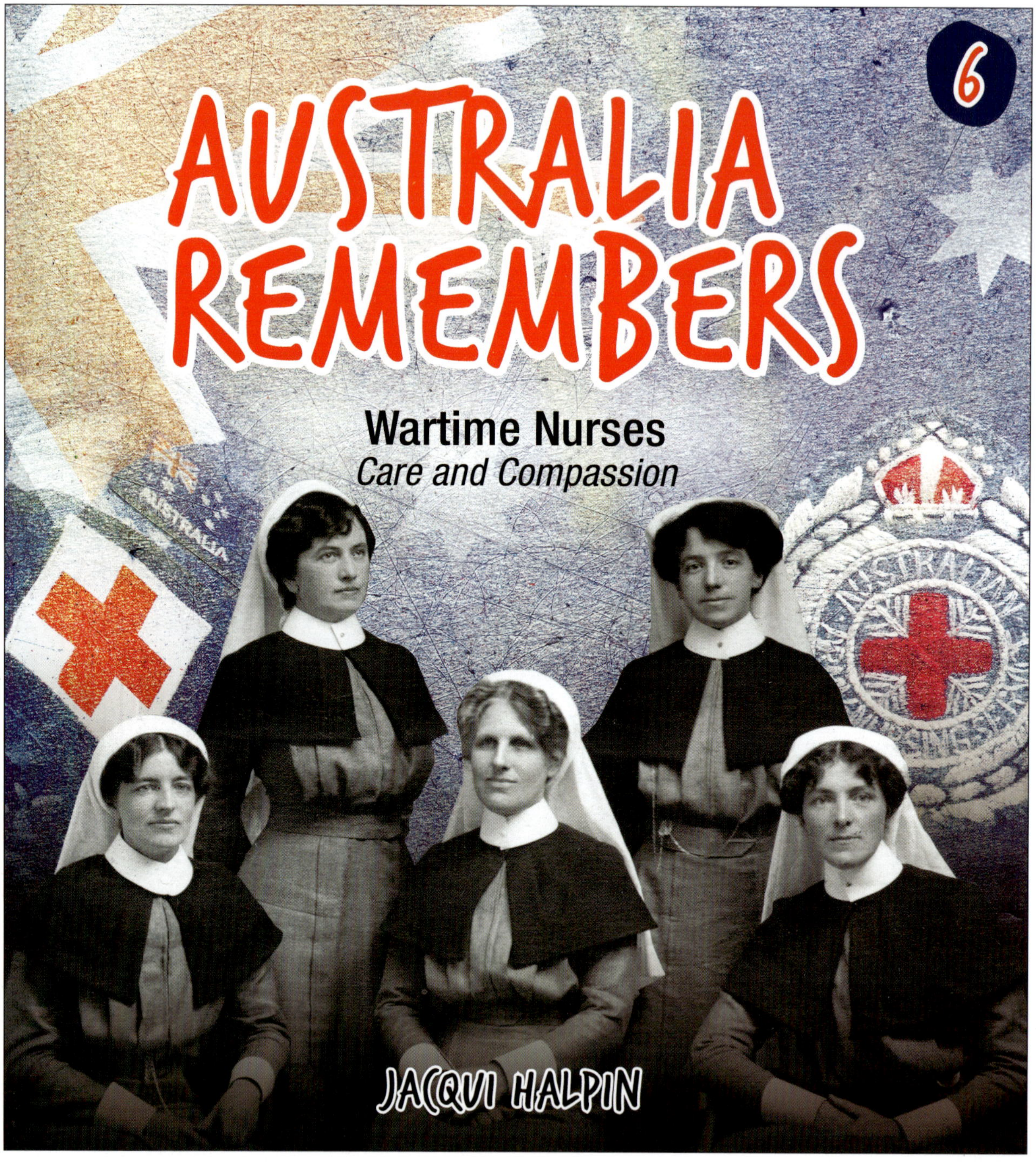

6

AUSTRALIA REMEMBERS

Wartime Nurses

Care and Compassion

JACQUI HALPIN

View sample pages, reviews and information on this book and other titles at **www.bigskypublishing.com.au**